FAERIES

Doorways to the Enchanted Realm

FAERIES

Doorways to the Enchanted Realm

Lori Eisenkraft-Palazzola

SMITHMARK

FAERIES

Doorways to the Enchanted Realm

This edition published in 1999 by SMITHMARK Publishers,
a division of U.S. Media Holdings, Inc.,
115 West 18th Street, New York, NY 10011

Project Director: Elizabeth Viscott Sullivan
Editor: Jean Mills
Concept & Idea: Janine Weitenauer
Design Team of 360 Degrees:
Anya Lemkova; Devorah Wolf;
Herta Kriegner; Shahira Youssef
Art Research: Anita Dickhuth.

SMITHMARK books are available for bulk purchase
for sales promotion and premium use.
For details write or call the manager of special sales,
SMITHMARK Publishers,
115 West 18th Street, New York, NY 10011; 212-519-1300

ISBN: 0-7651-1053-9
Printed in Hong Kong
10 9 8 7 6 5 4 3 2 1
Library of Congress CIP

Eisenkraft-Palazzola, Lori.
    Faeries : doorways to the enchanted realm / Lori Eisenkraft
-Palazzola.
        p.   cm.
    Includes bibliographical references.
    ISBN 07651-1053-9 (alk. paper)
    1. Fairies.   I. Title.
GR549. E39 1999
398.21—cd21   98-47856
                                       CIP

In loving memory of my father, **Ben Eisenkraft,**
who believed in all sorts of wee people, from Leprechauns
to the Whos in Whoville.

With much love to my mother and brother, for all
of their help, and for putting up with me.

To my husband, **Richard,** for never failing to believe in me.
May he find the right path and his way in life.

Acknowledgments

Special thanks to **Margaux King,** without whom this wouldn't have happened; **Steve Butler,** who good-naturedly, albeit under slight duress, read every draft during late evenings when manuscripts were thrust at him at Friday's, Santa Fe Steakhouse, and Regents Row; my sister-in-law, **Linda Eisenkraft,** for the occasional loan of Ben and Sam, whose every day is fantasyland; **Kelly Soong Too,** whose bridal shower I forgot to go to under tight deadline pressure; my mother- and father-in-law, **Grace** and **Frank Palazzolo,** and sister- and brother-in-law, **Donna** and **Paul Maggi,** who always believe in me, whatever I do; my forever friends: **Erika, Vicki, Kelly, Valerie, Ellen Sue, Lydia,** and **Natalie;** and my nephews, **Ben, Sam,** and **Alexander,** who are young enough to believe in the monsters and floating heads they see, the cartoon warriors they imitate, and the fantasies they have yet to learn. And, although this is not the way of the wee ones, I would like to thank the Faeries for the silver bracelet, glimmering feather, golden hand, and the odd black Faery cat. "God bless the Good Folk."

My gratitude goes out to **Devorah Wolf,** an excellent manager and designer, whose level-headed calm barely wavered—even under the most extreme conditions—and who was always available to discuss anything and everything under the sun; **Anya Lemkova**—designer extraordinaire—for her wonderful ideas, applications, and never-ending hard work; my editor, **Jean Mills,** for her help, enthusiasm, and cheerful good nature; **Anita Dickhuth,** for her photo research that turned up some of the most incredible images; and last, but certainly not least, **Janine Weitenauer** (and her water bottle), boss, art director, and fearless leader, who I am certain has Pixie connections.

table of contents

The

THE FAERY REALM

In a parallel world, alongside humankind, live the children of Nature—the **Daoine Sídhé**, the **Sith**, the **Tuatha dé Danann**, the **Twylth Teg**—the faery folk. We are all familiar with fairy tales—fantasies based on myth and folklore. However, this is not a book of silly stories or fantastic fiction. It is the history and truth of peoples whose chronicle spans a time long before ours began. And it is a history so ancient that long ago, what was real became legend, and truths turned to myth. Historians and scholars have pondered the puzzle of ancient civilizations for centuries, speculating and examining, discovering this, and discarding that. But in exploring the faery realm, it is important for us to seek out all things that have survived the mists of time. And what might these things be? What proof **is** there that the legendary faeries existed and still do?

There are very few ruins remaining, but there are some. And just because we have no great old faery cities to explore nor antiquated scrolls to scrutinize, no fossilized bones to examine nor deteriorating art to ponder, doesn't mean that faeries never existed—or that their descendants don't live on to this day. There are few ruins because the homes and castles that were built existed long before the empires of ancient Rome, Egypt, and Greece; and the dwellings of the faery folk, erected so many millennia ago, have long since crumbled into the earth. We have found no scrolls in ancient sandy caves, because they had no need to write. There are no curious sculptures to ponder, because nature was their artwork. And we have no bones because burial rites were primitive, to say the least. Whether the bodies of human races of faeries were simply buried in the earth under great cairns, or stones, or left for nature to decompose, most of their remains have long since turned to dust.

Scholars, however, have been able to relate the Bog people found late in this century to the prehistoric Celtic tribes—mortal faeries. As for the immortal faeries, though often humanlike, their physical makeup was not the stuff of ours.

Ultimately, what we need to examine is that which **does** exist: the factual and detailed stories passed down through generations, for oral history long preceded the written word. And from later centuries, the documents recorded from eyewitnesses. The faery culture is very much alive today, in many parts of the world, and there are firsthand accounts even now, in the late twentieth century, as well as places we can visit and examine ourselves.

Sidhé is Irish Gaelic, **sìth,** Scottish Gaelic, for "shee," meaning faery. **Sidheóg** means "little faery" and daoine **sidhé** means "faery people." Shee is also said by some lore to mean "spirit people," and it is also the word for the mound, dun, rath, burgh, or fortification of earth through which the faeries can enter and leave our world. Faery mounds are gate-

ways into the faery realm. The belief in some traditions is that the faeries are fallen angels or the souls of unbaptized babies unable to enter heaven: that is why they are sometimes called the spirit people. The word faery itself is said to mean enchantment, and originates from the Latin **fata,** meaning fate, a magical being, or one with magical powers.

Gaelic is the language of the ancient Celts, and thus the official faery language. Unless, of course, one encounters the Jinn (Genie) of Persia, in which case communication would likely take place in Arabic. But most of our knowledge of the faery world has come to us from such Celtic lands as Ireland, Scotland, Wales, the Isle of Man, Brittany, Devon, and Cornwall, and it is within these Gaelic-speaking countries that the very heart of Faeryland resides, and flourishes into the new millennium.

Called the Gentry, the Wee Ones, The Good People, and the Fair Family, depending on their country of origin, the stories of faery mystery and magic are still told today, so strong is their lure of

The belief in some traditions is that the faeries are fallen angels or the souls of unbaptized babies unable to enter heaven.

enchantment. And they are not just stories from a distant past, but evidence of faery magic happening all over the world today.

Not long ago, a young woman from Galway told me of a traditional Midsummer's Eve bonfire she had attended, and how the next day she and her family found a faery ring where none had been before. This is not surprising, as faeries are quite active around the ancient Celtic, or Pagan, holidays they celebrate. These include: Samhain (commemorating the start of winter and the new year, on November 1), Yule (festival of the winter solstice on December 21; a good time to look for the Holly King), Beltane (celebration of spring on May 1), and Midsummer's Eve (the most magical day of the year, on June 24). Every solstice and equinox is celebrated. All of these holidays are a time when the curtain between our world and the faery Otherworld is thinnest. They are the best occasions to catch sight of faeries, make wishes, and witness or make magic. If you're lucky enough to be in one of the countries where the Celts made their homes— especially Ireland, Scotland, Wales, the British Isles, and France, Belgium, and Northern Italy, which once comprised ancient Gaul—during a faery holiday, look for a faery ring. This may be a circle of grass darker than those blades around it, a ring of flowers or toadstools, or either of those surrounding a round dark green patch of grass. It is said these rings are formed by the faeries dancing about in a circle.

Throughout ancient history, we have myriad discrepancies on what happened when, why, and how. Among a group of people, each one recalls a different part of a story, sees things in a different light, and remembers or forgets an aspect selectively or inadvertently. History is patched together like the shards of an age-old Egyptian urn. The bits and pieces are glued together, and often, inevitably, chunks and snippets are irretrievably lost. This is also the case with the different traditions of faery lore. As history will always hold many and varied differences of opinion and interpretation, a host of versions of the same story, and different accounts altogether, the story of faeries is no exception. This book attempts to cover and weave together as much of that great and vivid diversity as possible.

Some people refer to the faeries as angels fallen from grace and others call them the undead. There are those who see them as of the spirit world, some who relate them to UFOs, and still more who believe they are the remnants of an ancient tribe of warrior people, with or without magical powers. The people to whom the latter refer are called the **Tuatha dé Danann,** Gaelic for the "Children, or Tribe, of the Goddess Danu." Danu is also known as the Anglicized Dana and the Welsh Dôn. The Tuatha are regarded as humans in ancient Irish history, although many people believe they were a race of gods and goddesses, and others accept that they were both. These warrior people are thought to have sailed to Ireland from their own lands in the east around the 15th century B.C.E. Landing there, they defeated and drove off the savage sea-monster Fomorians, the then inhabitants of Ireland, and called the place where they settled Tara. Many years later, the Tuatha were themselves defeated by the invading Milesians, who came from a land we know as modern-day Spain. The Irish today are said to be the descendants of this ancient people, who were related to the pre-Celtic tribes. The Milesians named the island they had conquered Éire, in honor of one of the three great Tuatha goddesses who battled them with powerful magic and valor. A queen as well as a goddess, her name was Ériu, and she is a great ancient heroine of Ireland. It is believed that the Tuatha dé Danann finally fled underground, building their palace and city beneath the earth, or vanished into the hills and caves of the countryside. Another theory is that they sailed across the sea and settled on another island. In any case, it is believed that they live in our world to this day.

The Tuatha dé Danann were an exquisitely beautiful, regal and graceful people who, as millennia passed, became relegated, or "demoted," to the designation of faery. They wore the most opulent finery and adorned themselves with wonderful handcrafted gold jewelry and gemstones. Their horses were of the purest white, they were magnificent in stature, and their manes and tails were bedecked with bells, jewels, and flowers, making them a true picture of equine royalty. The Tuatha were a race of nobles, gods and goddesses, perhaps, who had dealings with the kings, queens, and other titled and wellborn people of their time. They attended royal feasts and celebrations, participated in games of skill and hunts, and even, on the rare occasion, rode as these other rulers' allies in war. They practiced magic, shape-shifting, and Druidism. After they were conquered, the Tuatha disappeared, either underground, as described at left, or as some history tells us, they moved their kingdom to an island called **Tír Na Og,** or the "Land of Youth." While it was once held that the Tuatha dé Danann were a human race, and ancient Irish history documents them as early inhabitants of the island, scholars and historians are no longer certain. The Tuatha are often referred to as the Gentry, and are also known as **Sheagh Sidhé,** or the "Faery Host." All kinds of faeries like to gather at Tuatha burial sites for rituals and feasts.

12

When most people think of faeries, it is usually the tiny, winged sprite that comes to mind, but in fact, faeries have many different forms and sizes, and several do not have wings. Some appear humanlike, in both size and form, but the many different faeries are more diverse than we are.

Many faeries are quite curious about humans and like to eavesdrop on their conversations and daily activities. They often find our habits and lifestyles a great source of hilarity. However, they also tend to find us rather repugnant. Faeries are loyal, ethical, and sweet-natured. They dislike liars, oath-breakers, cheats, and those who can't keep a secret. They are known to place a curse on those who've broken a promise to them, and a faery damnation can span many generations. Faery curses are very difficult, if not impossible, to break. They also deplore infidelity, squalidness, cheapness, and the inconsistencies humans exhibit, as well as their poor treatment of animals and nature. And they don't like to be talked about behind their backs.

Faeries love decoration and adornment and often drape themselves in wreaths of flowers. Sometimes they add a crown of blossoms atop their heads as well, or an overturned bloom as a fragrant little cap. There are faeries who go about entirely naked and some that are dressed as peasants or nobility, while others may be covered with fur-like hairs or clothed in animal skins such as furs or leather.

Most faeries have abundant riches: golden, jewel-studded goblets from which to drink their wine, silver platters with which to elegantly dine, and a wide array of valuable treasures. These include such wonderful things as gold and silver, gem- and pearl-encrusted furnishings, necklaces, bracelets, rings, and anklets, jewels and trinkets, and baubles and beads. They especially adore emeralds. Some faeries have hidden treasure, such as a heap of gold coins, which they guard over much like the Leprechaun. And many faeries have lovely clothes of fine silk, brocade, and velvet.

Faeries love milk and cheese, bread and honey, butter, wine, and ale. They also like **uisge beatha**, Scotch Gaelic for "water of life"—in English: whiskey!—as well as apples, sweets, mouse soup, and tobacco, depending on the particular faery. Faeries who smoke pipes don't actually "smoke" them, for all of them hate smoke. Almost any of these things should be left as gifts for them if you hope to draw them near or simply welcome them. And, if you've received a faery favor, they do not want to hear words of thanks: it would only serve to offend them. This is not their way. A faery that takes always gives something back—particularly good fortune, riches, or magical gifts—and a faery that gives must be gifted in return, even if only a crust of bread.

If you have a reason to express gratitude to a faery, be sure to do so, else a nasty pinch, the loss of a possession, soured milk, or some other such faery prank will let you know you've been remiss. If you wish to meet a faery, you should gift him or her with some or other of the above-mentioned delicacies, little cakes, fresh water, or special, shiny or glittery stones, gemstones, or trinkets, which they favor as well. But never, ever leave even a tad of salt; faeries hate salt, as it is quite bitter and unpleasant to their palate.

A very important point to remember is this: gifts should be left for the faeries to find, and must never be handed to them directly. If the obviousness of your goodie is

made clear, the faery will disappear. Even worse, as in the case of the Brownie, a lack of proper etiquette will anger him. This may cause the grumpy little man to mutter abuses and make unpleasant mischief on his way out the door, never to return to what he considers such rude, insulting folk.

It is important not to offend faeries, for their rules are not the same as our own. Never call a faery by his or her given name. This will be perceived as a summons to appear and will give her power over

you, whereby she can spirit you away to Faeryland for evermore. It's also possible that calling a faery by name can give **you** power over **him.** In either case, it's best not to try to find out. Name taboos exist because some peoples believe that a given name holds much powerful magic and should not be used to call certain deities, royalty, or even family members, as it would be viewed as a challenge. Simply using the name Faery or Brownie will do.

Faeries adore children, and sometimes they steal them, often leaving in their place a changeling—a weak, unwell, or deformed faery child, or a feeble old faery—sometimes even a hunk of log under the bedclothes! Sadly, this may be because certain faeries are unable to have children themselves. On the other hand, some faeries just like stealing charming human moppets to keep for their own. Nevertheless, most faeries are keenly interested in joy and play, and are drawn toward laughter, games, music, and storytelling. They will happily amuse themselves by observing the fun, and will often join in with human younglings to participate in a merry chase or frolic, play hide-and-seek, or ring-around-the-rosy.

It has been said, time and again, that faeries would like nothing better than to sing and dance, and play and feast their days away, but this is not true for all of them, as plenty of them have work to do. And, considering that faeries can live anywhere from a few hundred to a thousand years or

more, they would become far too fat and lazy to do anything but feast some more!

However, certain types of faeries would never have time to accom-plish their tasks if they spent all the day long singing, dancing, and feasting on dainties. Flower faeries, for instance, each have their own flower to tend to and care for, from sunup to sundown. And likely an Elf or two assists her in the growing of and caring for the flower—from soil and seed to bud and bloom.

Seasonal faeries help with the changes to come, preparing the stuff of nature for the shift from winter to spring, summer to fall, and so on. Different faeries are active during particular seasons, and their time of year is evident in both the color and type of clothing they wear. For example, Autumn faeries dress in fall leaves of red, yellow, orange, and gold, while Yule faeries and Snow faeries are attired in furs and Yule faeries festoon themselves with holly leaves.

Water sprites and Fossegrim might play with you at a seaside retreat or waterfall, frolicking merrily and splashing about, while sea nymphs may help the lost seafaring soul find his way home or maliciously lead him to his death.

The **Bean Sidhé,** or Banshee, of Ireland has her own tasks, too. Often known as the Washer of the Ford, she can be found by the river washing blood-stained clothes. The Banshee can appear as an old hag or a lovely young woman, and has a particular family over whom she watches. Her woeful keening and mourning wail warns of coming death in

Autumn faeries dress in fall leaves of red, yellow, orange, and gold, while Yule faeries and Snow faeries are attired in furs and Yule faeries festoon themselves with holly leaves.

"her" family, most often one of the ancient families of Eire, though she appears in Scotland, too, where she is called the **Ban Sith.** It is said that when someone of great import is about to die, several Banshees may gather and wail together, in sorrow, mourning, and grief. As the saying goes, when one "wails like a Banshee" it is enough to instill dread even in the stoutest of hearts.

Then there are the merry Monaciello, or little monk, faeries of Calabria, Italy, who live in wine cellars. They are guardians who will watch over and protect your stores from any would-be thief of your wines. Not surprisingly, the Monaciello is always drunk, but he is a happy little sot and you should offer him a goblet of your finest by placing it on the cellar floor where he can find it.

Household faeries may visit your home, but not if it's dirty, messy, or otherwise unkempt (they adore lovely homes), and definitely not if a cat is in residence. Dogs, however, are quite fine indeed, and are often said to be a faery's familiar (companion, pet, friend)—especially a white dog. Faery dogs are easily identified, as they have long, pointy ears, much like Elves do. As the Welsh folk and people of many other cultures believe, white dogs themselves are fey creatures.

Faeries are known to be skilled weavers, and they turn out beautifully colored magical fabrics. Some of their material is used to make cloaks that render the wearer invisible, while other fabric is created to bind and magically heal wounds. Certain faeries are wonderful smiths. With talent and deftness, these metalworkers create exquisite jewelry, fine vessels, goblets, and platters, and tiny horseshoes for the little ponies that some of the faeries, especially Pixies, ride. There are faeries that are clever healers, and of other magical little people, the Elves truly are excellent shoemakers.

The great numbers of faeries bear no ill will; and above all, they respect fairness, honesty, and courage. However, there are certain faery groups and individual faeries that are known to be unkind, gruff, mean, or just plain malicious. These faeries may be classified as "dark," while their kinder brethren are known as "light" faeries.

The light faeries, such as the Seelies of Scotland, properly of the Seelie Court (the Blessed Ones), are "good" faeries, and their queen is sister to the queen of the Unseelie Court (the Unblessed or Damned). Unseelies are dark, malevolent faeries. According to some accounts, the Unseelies were originally part of the Seelie Court, a good-hearted and benevolent group of faeries who sparkle and glow as they ride the winds, looking for humans in need of help. It seems that long ago the Unseelies fell from grace due to their excessive pride and unkind, malicious ways. Perhaps we can look at them as sort of faery outlaws, as they ride the night winds, looking to inflict mischief upon the unsuspecting mortal.

Both the Seelies and Unseelies are the trooping faery sort. As opposed to solitary faeries, trooping faeries live, work, feast, play, and travel more as a family group, or extended family. A king and a queen rule trooping faeries and it is said that the trooping faeries are the fairest, most youthful and beautiful magical beings in the land.

Solitary faeries are just that. They are individual or one-of-a-kind faeries who are on their own. They may be young or old, good-looking or quite hideous, helpful or unkind, grouchy or merry, odd-looking or even headless. A good example of the solitary faery is the Ganconer, or love-talker. This handsome young male seduces milkmaids and other young women either with his incredible good looks or his enchantingly beautiful song. Women are said to pine for him unto death. It's not that the Ganconer is unfaithful; he's just being himself. The nature of this faery is to love them and leave them. His intention is not to bring harm, and his curse is to ultimately always be alone. He is undoubtedly a sad, lonely fellow. And unfortunately for certain young misses, the nature of the Ganconer's enchantment is powerful indeed.

Faeryland is a place where one never grows old. And there are many different versions of Faeryland. Maybe that's because there are a few different places where faeries make their homes. Some say it is a tremendous palace built within an ancient mountain, while others contend it is a mist-covered island visible only at night, or that it is an island, yes, but one that only rises out of the sea at dusk. It was once believed that the Isle of Man was one of these faery islands. Perhaps that's why belief is still so strong there. Other traditions hold that Faeryland exists underground, while different lore claims it is found underwater. It has also been referred to as Avalon, or "Apple Land," the Otherworld of eternal youth and immortality in Arthurian legend. Regardless of where Faeryland can be found, it is a mighty, multifaceted wonderland where all things are possible and all things exist.

One could visit Faeryland and find that it is summer all year round. Or perhaps you could wander through and pass all the different seasons on your way—from the fragrant new growth, dew, and luscious floral and green-grass scent of spring, the faeries' most favorite time of year, to crispy, apple-cinnamon-spicy, chrysanthemum-laden autumn, or glittery, snowflakey, peppermint winter.

There are strange and amazing beasts to be found in Faeryland, such as magical dragons, gryphons, and unicorns; heaps of gold and treasures, wonders, surprises, and a beauty and magic unknown by most of humankind. Even the flowers and rocks can speak in Faeryland. And faeries may live in a bit of Faeryland in our very own gardens, within a perimeter of enchantment. The wilder your garden grows, the better the faeries will like it.

In many ways, faeries are similar to humans. They work and play; they eat and sleep, have courts of justice, hunt and make war, and go about their daily business. They have individual personalities, traits, and skills just as we do, and they have feelings and moods like ours. But, there are great differences, too. Faeries make magic and mischief. Their values and beliefs are different than our own (and sometimes they are much nobler). True, their life spans equal many of our own generations, and the Woman of Lancashire is headless.

But most faeries are lovable and endearing, and I for one am the better for it when I find a Pixie peering out at me!

Faeries adore children, and sometimes they steal them, often leaving in their place a changeling...

The Stolen Child

Away with us he's going,
The solemn-eyed;
He'll hear no more the lowing
Of the calves on the warm hill-side.
Or the kettle on the hob
Sing peace into his breast;
Or see the brown mice bob
Round and round the oatmeal chest.
For he comes, the human child,
To the woods and waters wild,
With a faery hand in hand,
For the world's more full of weeping than
He can understand.

—William Butler Yeats, 1888

ENCHANTMENT

Faery glamour and faery enchantment are similar names for an array of magic that faeries can make. With glamour and enchantment faeries can become invisible, can shape-shift into other forms, such as beautiful humans, hideous beasts, grandmotherly figures, giants, animals, or trees, and can show mortals great wonders that don't really exist. Faeries are masters of glamorous illusion and wonderfully extravagant magic. For instance, a shabby little house can suddenly appear to be a magnificent castle; a warty-faced old sailor can turn into a handsome young prince. Humans see only that which the faeries want them to see, and if a faery wants to stay hidden altogether, she will. Further, if the faery wants you to believe that **she's** human, too, she may shape-shift into, or use faery glamour to appear as, a lovely innocent young woman.

Unfortunately for the faery, regardless of enchantment, if you've keen eyes and a sharp mind, likely you will notice he's got just one nostril, one finger less than he should, hooves instead of feet, or some other vague deformity that will give him away. But, more often than not, a faery will seem as you wish her or him: a fiery redhead with big blue eyes, a lovely, wispy, hazel-eyed brunette, maybe a blonde-haired, blue-eyed handsome youth, or a muscular, fine-featured warrior or knight. Trooping faeries are especially skilled with faery glamour, and faeries excel at creating all kinds of enchantments.

The Lorelei is a solitary faery who can be found in both Germany and England. She is a beautiful and bewitching young faery woman who lounges on rocky heights, particularly above the Rhine River, singing a song of enchantment. Sailors are seduced by her beautiful voice and are charmed to their death on the perilous rocks below her.

The Selkies of Scotland are also referred to as the Seal People. They have been caught in the act of shape-shifting from seal to human, and sometimes sport both beings' attributes at the same time. Selkies are said to be quite lovely and perfect in their human form, and often they enchant and lure mortals into their watery depths. Selkies, however, don't steal people. They seek only to find mates. And if a Selkie and a mortal fall in love, the faery seal can keep his human form and remain on land if he stays out of the sea long enough. Likewise, a mortal may wish to join the faery in her watery home, and with magical enchantment, the Selkie can turn her lover into one of the Seal People. Humans who have been turned into Selkies are easy to spot: they look like seals but have nearly human faces, as well as other, vaguely visible mortal features.

The **Leanhaun sidhé,** faery mistress, or faery sweetheart, is not the type of faery a gentleman would want to follow home. She can be found both in Scotland and Ireland, and the scope of enchantment she wields is great. The beautiful Leanhaun sidhé craves love, and tangles her lovers into a no-win situation. If her affections are refused, she indentures herself to her "victim" and badgers him without end. If the attention she desires is freely given, she gains all power over her lover, treating him like a slave and thriving off his life as he slowly dwindles to his death. This is not much of a problem for the malevolent faery mistress, as she takes herself off to find yet another young man to destroy.

Faeries can use the magic of their glamour to gift a homely young boy with the looks and stature of a handsome young man. However, for this there is likely a price to pay, else the faery will render the gift null and void. Then the young boy will have nothing but sad memories and little to show for such shallow endeavors. History tells that it is always best to keep your wits about you, lest the enchantment take you unawares and you fall prey to something you'll likely regret.

Sometimes faeries like to lure humans into Faeryland. Lovely young women are often taken, sometimes for marriage to a faery king, and handsome, virile men are unwittingly seduced silly into a world not their own. It has been written that when a mortal female marries a faery king, he keeps her for about seven years, or until she grows older and ugly! She is then returned to the human world with such gifts as the skill of healing or riches with which to support her cast-off self. This is the faeries' attempt at making up for her abandonment. Of course, sometimes the captured human is invited to stay in Faeryland, whether he has been lured there or simply stumbled in. He or she may then inter-marry if it is desired—and this must be acceptable to the faery's family and the faery king and queen, as well. Following this, the human is often magically made immortal. Sadly, if a faery who wishes to marry a human prefers to live in the mortal world rather than Faeryland, she may never return to her people and most, if not all, of her magical powers will be taken away.

23

Firsthand accounts warn to beware joining hands with faeries and dancing in a faery ring, for the steps will get faster as you whirl round and round, and your body will grow smaller and smaller to spritely proportions as you blissfully and ignorantly are spirited away to Faeryland. Once there, should you partake of faery food or drink, you will never be able to return to the human world. Sometimes, however, the faeries are sympathetic and will let you go home if you want to.

There are volumes of documentation from people who had been to Faeryland in the nineteenth century and earlier. According to them, entering Faeryland by other means—such as through a faery fort or mound or other gateway, and in one's human size and shape—could be a type of aid or protection in helping humans return to the mortal world. This may be because one entered uninvited or was not stolen away. However, the rule to avoid indulging in faery libations still stands. Should you decide to remain, or linger too long there, remember this: if once upon a fine day you decide to leave, you will not find the human world as you left it. Faery time is not the same as ours, and only days spent in Faeryland can be equal to many human years. When exiting Faeryland, the land of eternal youth, be prepared to lose the immortal beauty and strength you'd achieved by enchantment. Likely, you will find that you've aged to a humpbacked hag or a wizened old man, and all of your family and friends are long gone. Even worse, as soon as your feet touch the human earth, you may simply crumble away into dust.

Perhaps they wear their

Their chief occupations are *feasting, fighting,* and *making love,* and *playing* the most *beautiful music.* They have only one industrious person amongst them, the leprechaun— *the shoemaker.* Perhaps they wear their shoes out with *dancing.*

shoes out with dancing.

—William Butler Yeats, Irish Fairy & Folk Tales, 1892

MISCHIEF

Faeries in general are shy creatures and hide from humans. But there are always those that seek to stick their nose into human affairs, whether out of curiosity, amusement, or mischievousness. Many faeries have the ability to become invisible at will. This sets the stage for any number of pranks, such as listening in on private conversations, pinching or kicking grouchy people, and curdling milk. They also like rearranging humans' kitchen cupboards, "borrowing" their possessions, blowing out candles, and helping themselves to milk and honey. Other favorite pastimes include teasing mortals, as well as one another, hiding things, jumping and frolicking in hay, and keeping the baker's bread from rising. Faeries also enjoy playing practical jokes, startling humans, shape-shifting, and occasionally drinking to merry excess.

Pixies like to fly through the air in eggshells and ride about on their tiny ponies. They also enjoy using their magic to confuse travelers, helping them to become hopelessly lost. This is known as being Pixie-led. Although they giggle with glee over the confounded stranger in the forest, Pixies don't mean any harm. They just think it's a fun thing to do. It is believed that wearing one's coat or clothing inside out will protect the traveler from this faery mischief. Pixies also like to splash about in water and tap on walls to scare humans.

Faeries are whimsical creatures that ride about on pigs and chickens, fly through the air on flower stems and whatnot, and sail around in flower blossoms. They might free all the animals in the barnyard, kick you with a tiny foot if you're being stingy or mean, and gobble up all of your sweets. Faeries also like to dirty clean clothes drying on the line and are known to milk farmers' cows as they graze in the meadow. They delight in tangling or untying strings and rope, and take gleeful joy in mimicking humans.

People ought to remember that **egg-shells** are *favourite retreats* of the faeries, therefore the judicious eater should always **break the shell** after use, to prevent the *fairy sprite* from **taking up** his lodgment therein.

— Lady Jane Wilde, Ancient Legends, Mystic Charms, and Superstitions of Ireland, late 1800s

Not everyone is able to see faeries but oftentimes we can hear them. There is a story from Ireland, of people hearing wood being sawn, but when they went to investigate, all grew silent and no strangers were found lurking about. The sawing began again after the search had ended, and still, no other was found. Humans have heard wee voices singing and giggling, tiny hands drumming, rummaging, and tapping, but the noise-makers remained invisible. Is it because certain humans lack the heart to believe, or that the faeries choose to remain invisible to them— trusting some, but not many?

Perhaps the "second sight" or a special eye ointment the faeries concoct for just such a purpose is needed. Or a little mouse soup, which gives a mortal special wisdom and the ability to see the wee folk. Maybe it's just faery mischief, or it could be retaliation for disrespect, for which the faeries seek justice. They have been known to plague people for dumping water out the window upon their little heads, and faeries do not like humans building on their property and will demand the structure be dismantled. If you beg pardon and comply, likely they will gift you by telling of a better place to build, and you'll probably find gold and other riches when your digging there begins. Mind you, if you do not cease your building, the faeries will destroy it themselves.

When faeries steal some-thing from a human, they usually replace it with a gift. An item you've been missing for months or even years may suddenly turn up on your bureau, returned by the wee one that borrowed it. Often they just want to examine it. It is common knowledge among those with experience that when a faery borrows an item, a tool, or a gewgaw, it will be returned in perfect condition. And sometimes faeries happen upon an object that you've lost and will leave it in a place where you can find it.

Various means were employed to keep mischievous faeries from snatch-ing babies. Rowan branches or garlic could be attached to the cradle to ward off the wee people, and an iron horseshoe could be hung nearby to prevent the faeries from approaching an infant. Twisted bundles of ash, oak, and thorn twigs would also help, but if placed out individually, they would not have provided protection. Another way to foil a faery's attempt at abducting a child was to pre-tend that she or he was looked down upon with disfavor. A pretty little girl may have been given a hideous nickname on purpose, for faeries do not like anything that's ugly.

A freckle-faced laughing young boy may have been treated as useless to the family (though secretly loved dearly), for if the family didn't want him, the faeries wouldn't want him either. It was believed that if a child was treated "too well," the faeries would think he or she was someone quite special and spirit that little one away. Fickle, and sometimes vain and envious, if there's something you desire, the occasionally jealous faery will fancy it too.

Some who line to steal children are the Irish **Sheoques.** They live in ancient thorn bushes and faery forts surrounded by ditches, enjoy playing bagpipes, and like to enchant and steal children. In **Fairy & Folk Tales of Ireland,** W.B. Yeats mentions a letter that appeared in an Irish newspaper in the 1800s. According to the man who sent in the report, the Sheoques had taken a child, and the local priest had demanded the little one be returned.

The Sheoques did indeed return the youngster, unharmed and merry as could be. Faeries never harm children. Sometimes these same faeries abduct adults, too. They simply do not realize it is wrong to steal mortals, and it is quite sad to think of them wanting to keep humans for their very own, quite like a small child keeps a favorite stuffed teddy bear or a much-loved blanket by his or her side.

The beautiful Welsh **Twylth Teg,** or "Fair Family," used to steal children, and musicians, too. However, they are very kind and often more interested in gardening and working on their wild and colorful wonderland of flowers, trees, and shrubs. Many of them, in fact, live in flowers, such as foxgloves. Mischievous and friendly, they wear silk clothes, borrow cooking implements from humans, and enjoy music and dancing. The Twylth Teg have always been nice faeries and ask for nothing more than fresh water and viands.

Faeries' feelings are quickly hurt and they are easily offended or insulted. Many of them will go off and sulk, either because they have been misunderstood, been made to feel unhappy or sad, or something they treasure has been lost or taken away from them. It has been said that angry faeries can paralyze humans and cattle with faery darts, put damning curses that last for generations on those who've crossed them, and move into the homes of those who've abused them, behaving obnoxiously and refusing to leave. When an angry faery moves in, humans often must move out.

However, malevolent faeries usually steer clear of people, or at least that's so of the recent past. Records of ill-intentioned faeries have become few and far between of late, and perhaps this is due to a human attempt to glamorize them. It may also be that certain faery races have become extinct or are simply hiding. For information on warding off nasty faeries, see Chapter Four, Faery Encounters, page 74.

One of the faery family, the Pooka is an odd creature indeed. The **each visgé,** Gaelic for water horse, or sea horse, comes galloping out of the sea to run about on the land. He is a wild sea horse that can shape-shift into such animals as a bull or a goat, and those who manage to jump on his back in hopes of taming him end up on a madcap ride straight into a watery grave. The Pooka is rather a wise creature, however, who can speak to humans on November Eve, the first night of winter, on October 31. He provides intelligent conversation and can knowledgeably answer questions regarding predictions for the coming new year.

43

44

Sidhé gaoite is Gaelic for "faery blast," which is a gust of wind that can be caused by the Seelie Court flying past, faeries fighting among themselves, and faeries helping farmers with their chores in the hayfield.

A faery blast can turn into a gale strong enough to blow humans about, and even swipe the roof off of a house.

When peasants witness a sidhé gaoite, they usually murmur something protective, such as "God bless the Good Folk."

45

Var

VARIOUS FAERIES AND OTHERS

While the register of the many types of faeries seems nearly endless, and their traits and habits are quite diverse, there are still many standouts among the crowd. It's impossible to include the entire faery cavalcade, so here, instead, is a compendium of some of the most popular or obscure faeries known to humankind.

Dryads are happy, playful wood nymphs who live in, and take care of, trees. Usually born of the same seed that sprouted their home, Dryads can shape-shift into trees themselves. If you look very carefully at a Willow tree—the Dryads' favorite— you may be able to see the faery's face and body in the bark. But there are all kinds of tree nymphs, and they live in many countries, so one can look for them on other trunks as well.

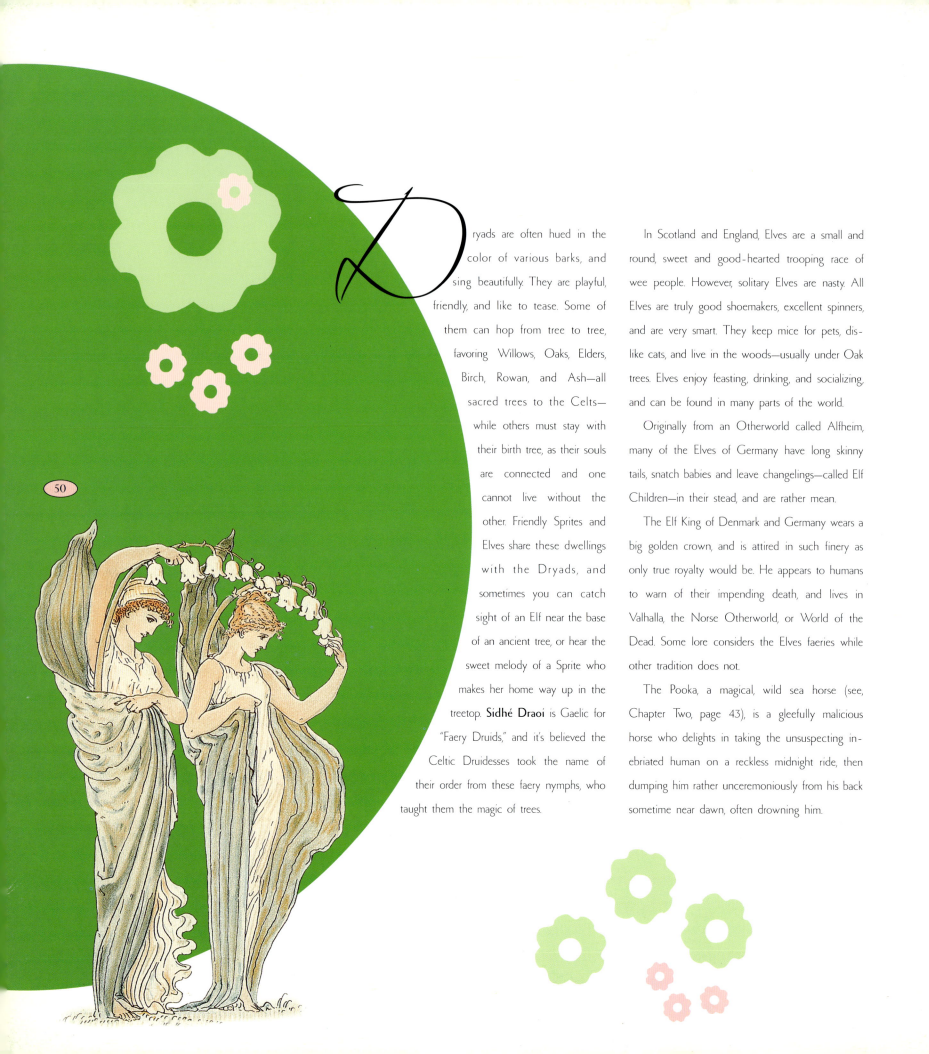

ryads are often hued in the color of various barks, and sing beautifully. They are playful, friendly, and like to tease. Some of them can hop from tree to tree, favoring Willows, Oaks, Elders, Birch, Rowan, and Ash—all sacred trees to the Celts—while others must stay with their birth tree, as their souls are connected and one cannot live without the other. Friendly Sprites and Elves share these dwellings with the Dryads, and sometimes you can catch sight of an Elf near the base of an ancient tree, or hear the sweet melody of a Sprite who makes her home way up in the treetop. **Sidhé Draoi** is Gaelic for "Faery Druids," and it's believed the Celtic Druidesses took the name of their order from these faery nymphs, who taught them the magic of trees.

In Scotland and England, Elves are a small and round, sweet and good-hearted trooping race of wee people. However, solitary Elves are nasty. All Elves are truly good shoemakers, excellent spinners, and are very smart. They keep mice for pets, dislike cats, and live in the woods—usually under Oak trees. Elves enjoy feasting, drinking, and socializing, and can be found in many parts of the world.

Originally from an Otherworld called Alfheim, many of the Elves of Germany have long skinny tails, snatch babies and leave changelings—called Elf Children—in their stead, and are rather mean.

The Elf King of Denmark and Germany wears a big golden crown, and is attired in such finery as only true royalty would be. He appears to humans to warn of their impending death, and lives in Valhalla, the Norse Otherworld, or World of the Dead. Some lore considers the Elves faeries while other tradition does not.

The Pooka, a magical, wild sea horse (see, Chapter Two, page 43), is a gleefully malicious horse who delights in taking the unsuspecting inebriated human on a reckless midnight ride, then dumping him rather unceremoniously from his back sometime near dawn, often drowning him.

51

.... it is best to stay on their good side, as they are easily offended.

If your interest lies with the trooping faeries, the most ornate and beautiful of all the wee ones, it's all the better if you've a doorway at either end of the house. These faeries will follow a path through your home in procession, some marching and dancing or playing miniature instruments, others riding their bell- and flower-bedecked faery horses and accompanied by fey dogs running alongside the parade, singing and drumming their way through one end and out the other. Likely they are on their way to a gathering or a feast.

The Abatwa are tiny, humanlike faeries who live in a tribal group among the anthills in South Africa. The only people who've seen the Abatwa are shamans, babies, and pregnant women. Kind-hearted and shy, these minia-ture clanspeople observe the same customs, beliefs, rituals, and feasts of the locals.

Some traditions lump all sorts of wee ones or magical beings under the faery banner while others most specifically do not. However, many of them are part of the faery kingdom nevertheless, and the majority of them can be found in Faeryland. In fact, some of them are great friends with, and work alongside, the faeries. The following is but a brief list of magical creatures that are likely not faeries per se, such as—but not necessarily including—Brownies, Elves, Gnomes, Trolls, Merrows Leprechauns, Ogres, Gryphons, Merpeople, Giants, Hobgoblins, and Pookas.

You are quite lucky if a house Brownie takes up residence in your home, for he will help with daily chores, wash and dry the dishes, bring in firewood, and even set the table. The Brownie will also take care of your pets, because he loves animals, and they adore him, too. All he desires in return are victuals and a warm place to sleep, preferably near the hearth. It is common knowledge that the house Brownie always enters and leaves through the chimney, but a Scotsman told me they'll use the front door as well. Brownies are certainly as helpful as can be, but beware if you are too good a housekeeper. If this constructive little man finds himself with no tasks to do: no cows to milk, no wood to chop, nor disorder to set to right, he will make a mess of your well-kept dwelling in the blink of an eye, thus creating some work for himself. Barring this, he will simply leave if you don't need him, and find someone who does.

Trows are Scottish Trolls that live in caves near the ocean or in sandy hillsides. Like the Scandinavian Trolls, they can be either dwarfs or giants. Generally, they are not nice at all, though some humans have befriended them. Both Trows and Trolls are dim-witted, unfriendly, and ugly. Trolls live in mountains or in castles, they sometimes kidnap people, and they cannot go out in the sun or they will explode or turn to stone.

Hobgoblins are mischievous, friendly, happy little magical beings that enjoy using their enchanting glamour. They like dancing and teasing, gifts of food and milk, and will do some housework and look after your young ones. Goblins, however, are mean. They are skinny and ugly, and break crockery and pound walls in the night to scare children. Both Hobgoblins and Goblins reside in France and England, and it is best to stay on their good side, as they are easily offended.

Gnomes are quite popular and are known throughout the world. Elderly little dwarf people, about one foot tall, they live to be about 1,000 years old. They can be found living with their spouses and children under ancient Oak trees in heavily wooded forests, and their magic protects and heals animals and humans. Gnomes wear pointy red hats and green clothes, are great friends with animals, and love to dance and have parties.

Water sprites might play with you at a seaside retreat,

frolicking merrily and splashing about,

while sea nymphs may help the lost seafaring soul find his way home,

or maliciously lead him to his death.

Faeries of the World

Folletti are tiny weather faeries whose feet face backwards. They live in **Italy** and mainly enjoy creating windstorms so they can glide through the air giggling merrily. Folletti also like to ride on grasshoppers and enjoy racing them.

Tiny, musically talented faeries called **Gandharvas** live in the forests, hills, and caves of **India.**

The **Chin-Chin Kobakama** is an elderly little Elf-like **Japanese** Brownie who may also reside in China. He likes to live in nice neat human homes, and protects the family there. All he requires is good housekeeping and tasty food.

Painajainen live in the **Alps of Europe.** Tiny, nasty white horses that trot through the mountains, these faeries

bring bad dreams to children and tease them mercilessly. Malevolent little equines, they can live for more than 3,000 years.

An **Irish** dandy, similar to other dwarfs, the **Clurichaun** sports elegant attire. Like the Italian Monaciello he, too, guards wine cellars and is usually drunk. A happy solitary faery who likes humans, he sings songs in Gaelic and asks for little more than food, wine, and friendship.

Alvens are water faeries that live in the **Netherlands.** They hate fish, like to float around in bubbles, and come on land to dance and play at night, when the moon has reached its peak. Not particularly friendly faeries, it is best not to swim with the Alvens.

The **Kelpies** of **Scotland** are little pointy-eared cannibalistic sea horses with manes and tails. These miniature monsters have big, sharp, pointy teeth, can shape-shift to lure their prey, and like to eat deer and humans, sometimes drowning them first.

Corrigans live in the woods and near streams in **Brittany** and **Cornwall.** They are winged faery Druidesses who like to play pranks, tease Christians, for Corrigans are pagans, and run off with mortal babies, leaving changelings in their stead.

Norway is the homeland of the **Fossegrim.** They live near waterfalls, sing beautifully, and carry their mischief just a bit too far. Lovely, miniature human-like faeries, Fossegrim have no feet.

Merrows are **Irish** Merpeople. Top half humanlike, bottom half fish, fishermen say that male Merrows have green hair and green teeth, pigs' eyes, and red noses. Female Merrows are said to be quite beautiful, with long green hair which they sit upon rocks to comb, much like Mermaids do. The Merrows are happy and gleeful, frolic in the water, and live in old shipwrecks. They have rescued many drowning humans and helped direct lost ships home. Merpeople, on the other hand, are not so nice. Mermaids are known to sit on rocks to comb their long blonde hair, sing lovely songs, create foul weather, and lure sailors to their death.

Naked little trooping faeries called **Callicantzaroi** ride about on chickens in **Greece** and **Italy**. They each have the feet of a different animal, and enjoy celebrating the Yule holiday with much revelry, feasting, and glee.

Clim is the name of a mischievous **Goblin** who resides in the chimneys of **Sussex,** in **England.** There, this tiny one peeks out at children who are studying or playing, and scolds them when they become unruly.

The tiny **Welsh Ellyllon** are trooping faeries who adore toadstools, silk clothing, and mortal children. They live on little islands and in the hills of Wales, where they keep herds of little faerie cows.

Austria is the home of the nasty little fellow called **Krampus.** Reputedly a Christmas Elf, this solitary, boggle-eyed wee one travels about on winter nights, looking for unpleasant children to punish.

The **Lutin** of **Normandy** are prankster Elves who enjoy frolicking with human children, braiding and snarling the tails and manes of horses, helping with farm chores, and playing pranks on mortals.

The story of the **Swedish Tomte Gubbe** is similar to that of the Tuatha dé Danann. Once a people of great magic and wonder, these original inhabitants of Sweden were forced underground when the Vikings invaded their land. Many years later, they became known as faeries.

The **Vala** are beautiful little trooping faeries that can be found in the forests of **Eastern Europe**. They are healers and guardians of the woods and streams, and they love playing music and dancing.

The **Domoviks** are **Russian** house Brownies. Wizened little old men with long gray beards, they are family and household guardians who finish undone tasks late at night, warn of impending danger, and occasionally cause mischief. Domoviks like to make their bed near the warm kitchen stove and enjoy the hot meal which is left for their supper.

63

FAERY ENCOUNTERS

Although faery sightings are much less common today, there are many good places to look for them, as well as for doorways into their lands. For your search to be fruitful, it is important that you possess fine qualities or the faeries will avoid you, perhaps even scorn you. Certainly you will not have any sort of happy faery experience if you are ill-willed, grumpy, mean, nonbelieving, or spiteful. You must be good at heart, kind and gentle, open-minded and relaxed, and, most especially, respectful. A subtle curiosity is okay, too. Any lands of the ancient Celts are excellent to begin such a quest. So, too, are the countries of Scandinavia, the Netherlands, Asia, Eastern Europe, Austria, Germany, Switzerland, Italy, Greece, Iceland—the list is vast. The following will make it easier for one to find and meet faeries.

Faeries favor wild, undeveloped areas. The best places to look are in forests, the countryside, meadows, caves, and mountains. Undeveloped terrain—those places still untouched or little marred by humankind—are the ones you need to seek. Remember that such locales exist in North America and South America, too.

A search for faeries may be conducted at any place and time where two points meet: where the sea meets the beach, mountain meets land, or woodland meets meadow. And be sure to look for places where the ancient world meets the new: old ruins, aged boulders, standing stones, age-old trees, and more, at just about any time of year, but particularly around faery holidays. Another good time is spring, for it is the faeries' favorite season. Look for them in caves and on hillsides, near streams and in flowers and trees.

ore "places" that two points converge are certain times of day: these are at dawn, noon, sunset, and midnight.

Wander around until you feel you have found a good place. If you are unsure, wander a bit more. Leave your mind open; be happy, light-hearted, and merry as you troll about. If you don't find a place you feel is "just right," then you are probably trying too hard, and blocking out any attempts to guide you. It need not be the perfect place. There are many places. If you can't find any faeries, it may be that they don't want you to.

If you **do** find a faery mound, a wondrous cave, a giggling brook, or perhaps an old castle, manor house, or cottage ruins, that will be great good luck for you. If you discover a faery ring, or have a feel-ing about a special stone or tree, keep a respectful distance and peacefully settle nearby. Remember to walk around standing stones, faery rings, and faery mounds rather than across or through them. This is disrespectful. Sit or lie quietly in the grass and lose yourself. Breathe in the fresh, clean, fragrant air. Inhale the scent of wildflowers, grass, soil, and trees. Listen to birdsong, gentle breezes, and the rustle of leaves. Let yourself become one with nature.

If you should discover a faery ring, the best time to see the faeries dancing is under a full moon or near midnight on the eve of a faery holiday. Quietly and kindly, situate yourself at a distance. Faeries do not like to be spied on, although they may spy on you! If you are lucky, you may see them dancing around the ring, twirling and leaping, sometimes holding hands, sometimes not, their bodies and tiny crowns wreathed in garlands of flowers.

Miniature musicians playing flutes, fiddles, harps, or bagpipes accompany their sweet, high voices trilling song. Often the ethereal faery queen sits in the center of the ring, watching over her family. Bathed in moon glow and dressed in a white flowing gossamer gown, she is adorned with flowers and jewels and possesses a beauty no human is blessed with. She also guards the secret of hidden treasures.

The Fairies

Up the airy mountain

Down the rushy glen,

We daren't go a-hunting

For fear of little men;

Wee folk, good folk

Trooping all together;

Green jacket, red cap

And white owl's feather.

— William Allingham

Bard of Ballyshannon, Donegal, Ireland, 1850

If you play an instrument that faeries like, such as a flute or a recorder, it is a good idea to sit there and play sweet music. Try a guitar, too, but play softly and soulfully or with gladness and joy. Faeries don't like loud noises and can be frightened off by the sound. If you've a lovely singing voice, then sing gentle, happy songs. If you have a tin ear, never mind, then. Faeries can't bear listening to a tuneless human and will cover their pointy little ears with their tiny hands, ape you, and pelt you with pebbles. Storytelling is a good idea, as they will come and listen to a tale if you tell it aloud. All of these things will help lead the faeries to you.

Remember that faeries do not like "invasions." One farmer who entered a faery market uninvited was pushed and shoved by the crowd until he finally emerged bruised and with a lame leg as a lifelong reminder that faeries do not like intruders. Let your kind presence not be an invasion of privacy, but one of good-willed curiosity. Do not approach any faeries unless you are invited, and, unless a faery speaks to you, it is up to you, to make a judgement call in initiating a conversation. Some solitary faeries may be jealous, mean, and spiteful. Steer clear of them. If a brief encounter is unavoidable, give a quick nod or salute of recognition and go on your way. Never run away from a faery, as it will only be an enticement for him to chase you. If you sense danger and cannot swiftly move away, you'll need to utilize a little mental agility. Do not be defensive and don't show any fear. Do be kind but sharp-witted. Talk to her a bit if you like, gift her with a trinket, then quickly bid her a good day, and be on your way.

e sure to prepare in advance for your faery search. Some items to bring include snacks—for yourself and any faeries you may chance to meet—little cakes, fresh water, and sweets are especially good. Bring your instrument, if you play one, perhaps a nice tartan blanket to sit down on, a few trinkets for gifts, some salt, and a piece of iron (a horseshoe or nail will do nicely) for emergencies. If you should inadvertently call a malevolent or trickster faery to you, the best defense would be to brandish the iron horseshoe. Faeries hate iron because it can temporarily take away their powers, so this should protect you and keep little nasties away. And keep the salt handy. If there's time, quickly pour it in a ring around you. Faeries hate salt and it's a line they will not cross.

Since faeries are shy and usually hide, it may take some time to coax them out. Often, one may come upon them simply by chance. They can use their magic to become invisible or they can hide and blend in with trees, flowers, or rocks, depending on the type of faery. If you hear faeries but can't find them, ask if you may see them. You must languish with an air of nonchalance, sometimes for quite a long while. Meanwhile, read a book or contemplate, and watch the trees and shrubs, flowers and grass for any movement, such as a tiny eye blink or a sparkle of Pixie dust. Also, listen hard for small sounds such as a whisper, giggle, or sigh. Faeries like to observe and eavesdrop. If you feel you are being watched, you probably are.

Do not approach any faeries unless you are invited. And, unless a faery speaks to you, it is up to you to make a judgement call in initiating a conversation.

GOOD FORTUNE

The great majority of faeries represent goodness and honesty. They have noble qualities and higher values than most humans do. Faeries are kind and compassionate; they protect women, children, and animals, and have a high regard for nature and beauty. The Fair Folk impart knowledge and wisdom to humans they deem deserving, and leave gifts for people who honor and respect them. According to Irish lore, faeries have much knowledge of herbs and healing and will find a way to guide humans to the treatment they require. They lead miners to veins rich in metals and gems, will watch over your home, and help with daily chores. They pinch and prod the lazy, lead thirsty people to water, and take care of animals. Playful and giving, mischievous and merry, their standards are admirable and their hearts are in the right place.

*F*aeries have helped humans mend broken hearts and broken dreams, and have relieved depression and sadness with both the material and emotional gifts they bring. Favored humans are granted good luck, warned of coming disaster in an attempt to help thwart it, and are sometimes led to a pot of gold or other treasures. Faeries rescue drowning sailors, guide lost travelers home, feed the hungry, and bring happiness and fantasy back to the jaded. Faeries can grant wishes and make dreams come true. The only requirements are that one respects and believes.

*I*t is well known that when faeries choose a cow to milk, the farmer who owns the beast will always enjoy the most wonderful milk from this faery-blessed cow. Faeries will reward people who protect and respect wildlands and nature, and will gift those who care for sick or frightened animals. They will always return to humans in kind that which is given solely and completely from the heart. You may find a simple handmade silver bracelet or an unusual golden ring on your kitchen counter one morning, and not know where it came from. Even more surprisingly, it fits perfectly. Probably it was left for you by the curious little pointy-eared man dressed in animal skins and a red cap who stopped at your door the night before, seeking a warm fire near which to warm his cold little toes.

enehunas are dwarf-like tropical Elves garbed in traditional native attire. They live in the jungles of Polynesia, and guard a mound of treasure. If you capture a Menehuna, you are granted a wish. These magical little people live near waterfalls and help lost humans find their way out of the jungle, taking them to a cool place to rest and fortifying them with libations first.

The magical Jinns (Genies), or Bottle Imps, of Persia are a lucky find, indeed, providing good fortune to anyone who uncorks the bottle or rubs the lamp. These cooped up wish-granters originally belonged only to sheiks and other powerful rulers, and if a bottle or lamp was discovered missing, an army was sent out to retrieve it. Jinns are great mischief makers. They can shape-shift into giants, make themselves hideously ugly, and sometimes have the feet of a camel.

Sweet-natured and gentle, faeries do not hurt anyone whom they steal and have been known to leave toys for children. These pranksters and mischief makers also leave clothes, food, and alms for the poor. They guard wine cellars, place protective wards on the humans they like best, and magically make dough rise and butter churn. Faeries have lived alongside and helped humans for hundreds of years. Long ago, during the times of the Pagans and on into the nineteenth century, humans and faeries used to interact on a daily basis. Before cultural and industrial revolutions and high-tech modernity, humans often sought out faeries for their good advice and predictions and to request magical charms and counteraction of spells. In those days, mortals and faeries were often friends, and the wee ones felt free to borrow what they needed from farmers and housewives. They rewarded these people by giving good fortune, breaking spells placed on mortals by witches, and giving them bowls of food that never diminished. They have gifted humans with magical cloth, beautiful jewels, gold coins, good deeds, and more.

Faeries bring out the child in each of us, that long-forgotten little one who wants to play and find joy and wonder with each new day. They restore our sense of curiosity and adventure and encourage silliness and laughter. Faeries remind us that there's a fine line between fact and fantasy and myth and truth. Are they or are they not a forgotten race, living in a realm beside our own? They have been seen and heard at work and play for many hundreds of years, and even today, belief in them still flourishes in many parts of the world.

I know the faeries are there now, dancing in Ireland and Scotland, making mischief in the Highlands, and singing on the Isles of Man and Skye. They are gardening in Wales and traipsing about Brittany, lounging and feasting in Devon and Cornwall, and riding the winds in Italy. And when I smell flowers that aren't there or hear wind chimes that don't exist jingling in the breeze, I know the wee ones are hailing me, and playing somewhere quite nearby.

I know
the wee
ones are hailing
me, and playing
somewhere

quite
nearby.

bibliography

Andrews, Ted.
Enchantment of the Faery Realm.
St. Paul, Minn: Llewellyn Publications, 1997.

Bord, Janet.
Fairies: Real Encounters with Little People.
New York: Dell Publishing, 1997.

Clarkson, Atelia, and Gilbert B. Cross.
World Folktales.
New York: Charles Scribner's Sons, 1980.

Cohen, Daniel.
Monsters, Giants, and Little Men from Mars.
Garden City, NY:
Doubleday and Company, Inc., 1975.

DeLys, Claudia.
**What's So Lucky About
a Four-Leaf Clover?**
New York: Bell Publishing Company, 1989.

Green, Miranda J.
Dictionary of Celtic Myth and Legend.
London and New York:
Thames and Hudson, 1992.

Haining, Peter.
The Leprechaun's Kingdom.
New York: Harmony Books, 1979.

Jobes, Gertrude.
**Dictionary of Mythology,
Folklore and Symbols.**
New York: The Scarecrow Press, Inc., 1962.

Jones, Alice.
Larousse Dictionary of World Folklore.
Edinburgh and New York:
Larousse Kingfisher Chambers Inc., 1995.

Leach, Maria, ed.
**Funk & Wagnall's Standard Dictionary
of Folklore, Mythology and Legend.**
New York: Funk & Wagnall's Company, 1984.

McHargue, Georgess.
**Impossible People: A History
of Natural and Unnatural Beings
Terrible and Wonderful.**
New York: Holt, Rinehart and Winston, 1972.

MacLiammóir, Micheál and Eavan Boland.
W.B. Yeats and His World.
New York: A Studio Book, Viking Press, 1972.

McCoy, Edain.
A Witch's Guide to Faery Folk.
St. Paul, Minn: Llewellyn Publications, 1997.

Moura, Ann.
**Green Witchcraft: Folk Magic,
Fairy Lore & Herb Craft.**
St. Paul, Minn: Llewellyn Publications, 1997.

Mynne, Hugh.
The Faerie Way.
St. Paul, Minn: Llewellyn Publications, 1996.

Rose, Carol.
**Spirits, Fairies, Leprechauns,
and Goblins: An Encyclopedia.**
New York: W.W. Norton & Company, 1996/98

Stiles, Eugene.
A Small Book of Fairies.
San Francisco: Pomegranate Artbooks, 1995.

Wilde, Lady.
Ancient Legends of Ireland.
New York: Sterling Publishing Co., Inc., 1996.

———.
Irish Cures, Mystic Charms & Superstitions.
New York: Sterling Publishing Co., Inc., 1991.

Yeats, William Butler, ed.
Irish Fairy & Folk Tales.
New York: Boni & Liveright, 1888, 1918;
New York: The Modern Library, 1994.

s o u r c e s

The wonderful specialty shop **Enchantment** has an on-line catalog featuring hand-painted resin Flower Faeries™, one-of-a-kind Faeries, Pixie teapots, Faery jewelry, and blown-glass Pixies and Faeries. They also feature Faery books, note cards, clocks, and lots more. Stop by the enchantment Web site at http://home.earthlink.net/~faeries, or write for more information:
Enchantment
The Merchants Mart
2411 Main Street
Santa Monica, CA 90401

Gael Force Imports offers a wealth of Celtic goods from such places as Ireland, Scotland, and the British Isles. Visit their Web site at www.gaelforce.com to order Celtic books, jewelry, and giftware, as well as Celtic art, edible goodies, and clothing.

Llewellyn Publications has a combination book catalog/New Age magazine featuring many nonfiction books on the subject of Faeries and the ancient Celts. To request a single copy of **Llewellyn's New Worlds of Minds & Spirits** call (800) THE-MOON, check out their Web site at www.llewellyn.com, or write to them at:
Llewellyn Publications
P.O. Box 64383
St. Paul, MN 55164-0383
A yearly, bimonthly subscription of six issues costs $10.

An enchanting array of Faery and Celtic jewelry, other magical motif accessories, such as pendants, bracelets, earrings, and more, and exquisite Faery mirrors, are available from **Open Circle Distributors.** Send a check or money order for $2 (refunded with order) to:
Open Circle Distributors
1750 East Hill Road #G
Willits, CA 95490
You can also phone to order a catalog, (800) 726-8032, or stop by their Web site at www.ancientcircles.com.

Signals is a mail-order catalog that offers a number of Celtic items, from jewelry and CDs to a framed lucky four-leaf clover. For a free catalog, call their catalog request line at (800) 570-1004.

Celtic jewelry, videotapes, and CDs, as well as jewelry and plaques with Gaelic inscriptions and flower jewelry can be found in **Wireless.** The catalog also offers Irish and Scottish books, CDs, crystal, and instruments. For their free mail-order catalog, phone (800) 570-5003.

Unique and irresistible pewter and hand-painted Faeries can be mail-ordered from **The Wizards Way.** Check out their on-line catalog at www.wizardsway.com to see lovely little seasonal, wood, and magical Faeries and Pixies, or call them at (888) 282-0002.

Dunraven House has a variety of Celtic magic and Faery-related items, such as Faery dust, candles, and Faery spell kits. A catalog costs $2 (refunded with order):
Dunraven House
P.O. Box 403
Boulder, CO 80306

Folk museums can be found throughout the world, and likely, you can find one in your own city or town, or somewhere nearby. However, the four below are real standouts, and if you have the opportunity, you may want to visit one of the following:

Folk Museum of Glencolumbkille
County Donegal, Ulster
Ireland

Märchen und Wesersagen-Museum
(Museum of Fairy Tales and Weser Legends)
Am Kurpark 3, D-4970
Bad Oeynhausen, Nordrhein-Westfalen
Germany

Norsk Folkemuseum
Museumsveien 10
Bygdøy N-0287
Oslo, Norway

Welsh Folk Museum
St. Fagans
Cardiff, South Glamorgan
Wales

photo credits

Cover, 1 • From **The Elf King's March of the Triumph,** by Richard Doyle/ Mary Evans Picture Library; 2 • From **The Princess Nobody** by Richard Doyle/ e.t. archive; 3 • From **The Elf King's March of the Triumph,** by Richard Doyle/Mary Evans Picture Library; 6 • From **Olaus Magnus de Gentribus Septentrionalibus/**e.t. archive; 8 • **The Fairy Lovers** by Theodore von Holst, The Tate Gallery, London/Art Resource; 11 • **Fairy Ring** by Arthur Rackham/Mary Evans Picture Library/Arthur Rackham Collection; 12/13 • Illustration by Amelia Jane Murray, Lady Oswald/Christie's Images; 14 • **Autumn** by John Atkinson Grimshaw, Roy Miles Gallery, London/The Bridgeman Art Library, London & New York; 16 • Illustration by Warwick Goble/Mary Evans Picture Library; 18 • **A Midsummer Night Dream**/Mary Evans Picture Library/Arthur Rackham Collection; 20/21 • Edouard Zier in **Journal des Voyages,** 1899/Mary Evans Picture Library; 22/23 • **Fairies Dancing Inside a House** by S. Meteyard/Mary Evans Picture Library; 24/25 • **The Fairy Twilight** by John Austen Fitzgerald/Christie's Images; 26/27 • **A Fairy Resting Among Flowers,** by Amelia Jane Murray, Lady Oswald/Christie's Images; 28/29 • **An Elfin Dance** by Richard Doyle/Christie's Images; 30 • R.M. Euchler in **Jugend,** 1898/Mary Evans Picture Library; 32/33 • **Wood Elves Hiding** by Richard Doyle/Art Resource; 35 • Unnamed artist in **Svenska Folksagner,** 1882/Mary Evans Picture Library; 36 • Lercche, in Norsk Kunstner-Albumkle, 1872/Mary Evans Picture Library; 39 • Gustav Tenggren in Good Housekeeping, 1920s; 40/41 • **The Frog Bandits** by Beright Henry Barnabus/Christie's Images; 44 • Florence Mary Anderson in **Little Folks,** 1917/Mary Evans Picture Library; 45 • From **The Elf King's March of the Triumph,** by Richard Doyle/ Mary Evans Picture Library; 46/47 • From **The Princess Nobody,** illustration by Richard Doyle/e.t. archive; 48 • **A Fairy Resting on a Shell** by Amelia Jane Murray, Lady Oswald/Christie's Images; 50/51 • (both) From **Flora's Feast,** by Walter Crane, 1889/AKG London; 53 • **Goblins and Toadstools** by Arthur Rackham/e.t. archive; 54 • **The Fairy Teller's Stroke** by Richard Dadd. Tate Gallery, London. Photo by John Webb/e.t. archive; 57 • From **Andersen's Fairy Tales,** illustration by Arthur Rackham/Mary Evans Picture Library; 58 • Illustration by Arthur Rackham for Milton's **Comus**/Mary Evans Picture Library/Arthur Rackham Collection; 60/61 • **The Fairy's Lake** by John Austen Fitzgerald. Tate Gallery, London/Art Resource; 64 • Claude Shepperson in **Princess Mary's Gift Book**/Mary Evans Picture Library; 66/67 • **Ariel** Illustration by Arthur Rackham to **The Tempest**/Mary Evans Picture Library; 68/69 • Florence Anderson, in Lady Margaret Sackville's **The Travelling Companions**/Mary Evans Picture Library; 70 • **Goblin Market,** illustration to Christina Rossetti's poem "Warwick Goble" in **The Book of Fairy Poetry**/Mary Evans Picture Library; 73 • **A Swedish Nisse Surprises a Girl in her Bedroom,** 1882/Mary Evans Picture Library; 74/75 • Theodor Kittelsen in **Asbjornsen,** 1887/Mary Evans Picture Library; 76/77 • **A Traveler Encounters a Water Nymph** by Helen Stratton/Mary Evans Picture Library; 78/79 • **Faery Twilight** by W. E. Frost/Mary Evans Picture Library; 80 • **Robin Goodfellow, A Sprite** by Charles Folkard in **The Children's Shakespeare**/Mary Evans Picture Library/The Folkard Collection; 83 • **The Gnomes**/AKG London; 84/85 • **Landscape with Magic Procession** by Girolamo da Carpi/Scala/Art Resource; 86 • "Wag at the Wa," 1866/Mary Evans Picture Library; 88 • **Elves Dancing in a Ring,** circa 1890/Mary Evans Picture Library; 90/91 • **Language of Flowers,** 1884 by Kate Greenaway/e.t. archive.

index